We the People

W9-CIM-513

The Declaration of Independence

by Michael Burgan

Content Adviser: Professor Sherry L. Field,
Department of Social Science Education,
College of Education, The University of Georgia

Reading Adviser: Dr. Linda D. Labbo,
Department of Reading Education,
College of Education, The University of Georgia

Compass Point Books ✦ Minneapolis, Minnesota

Compass Point Books
151 Good Counsel Drive
P. O. Box 669
Mankato, MN 56002-0669

 This book was manufactured with paper containing
at least 10 percent post-consumer waste.

Photographs ©: North Wind Picture Archives, cover, 4; Archive Photos, 5, 6, 7; FPG
International/Photoworld, 9; Archive Photos, 10, 12 top and bottom, 13; FPG International, 14;
North Wind Picture Archives, 15; Archive Photos, 16; North Wind Picture Archives, 17, 18, 19;
Archive Photos, 21; Archive Photos/Joe Griffin, 23; North Wind Picture Archives, 24, 27, 28;
Archive Photos, 29, 32; Visuals Unlimited/C.P. George, 33; Archive Photos, 35, 37; North Wind
Picture Archives, 38, 39; Archive Photos, 41.

Editors: E. Russell Primm and Emily J. Dolbear
Photo Researcher: Svetlana Zhurkina
Photo Selector: Dawn Friedman
Design: Bradfordesign, Inc.
Cartography: XNR Productions, Inc.

Library of Congress Cataloging-in-Publication Data
Burgan, Michael.
    The Declaration of Independence / by Michael Burgan.
        p. cm. — (We the people)
    Includes bibliographical references and index.
    Summary: Examines the political situation in America at the time of the troubles between
England and her colonies there and describes how the Declaration of Independence was written
and accepted.
    ISBN 978-0-7565-0042-9 (hardcover)
    ISBN 978-0-7565-0938-5 (paperback)
    1. United States. Declaration of Independence—Juvenile literature. 2. United States—
Politics and government—1775–1783—Juvenile literature. [1. United States. Declaration of
Independence. 2. United States—Politics and government—1775–1783.] I. Title. II. We the
people (Compass Point Books).
    E221 .B945 2000
    973.3'13—dc21   00-008671

Visit Compass Point Books on the Internet at *www.compasspointbooks.com* or e-mail your request
to *custserv@compasspointbooks.com*

TABLE OF CONTENTS

A Decision about Independence

On June 7, 1776, members, or delegates, from the thirteen American **colonies** gathered in Philadelphia. They met at the Pennsylvania State House (now Independence Hall).

These men formed the Second Continental

Independence Hall in Philadelphia

Congress. The colonies were rebelling against Britain and its king, George III. The Congress now had to decide whether America should declare its independence. It was a very important decision.

George Washington in 1775

Fighting between the colonists and British troops broke out in April 1775 in Massachusetts. The Continental Congress then named General George Washington commander of the American troops. His soldiers had already won the Battle of Bunker Hill.

The British had held off an American raid in Canada and were now preparing for an attack

5

along America's East Coast. And spies in London, England, had learned that King George had hired foreign troops to fight in America.

The delegates of the Continental Congress discussed their next step. The colonists had mixed feelings about declaring independence from Britain. About one-third of the American people wanted independence. About one-third believed the

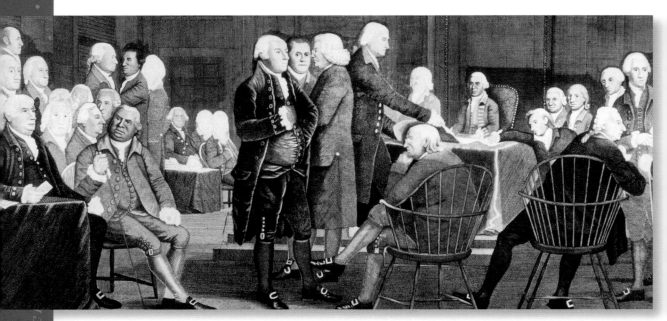

The delegates of the Continental Congress

colonies should remain under British rule. The rest couldn't make up their minds.

Richard Henry Lee

The delegates in Philadelphia were also unsure, but they knew time was running out. They had to make the decision.

Richard Henry Lee of Virginia rose and addressed the Congress. He presented a **resolution**, or statement. It said, "that these united colonies are, and of right ought to be, free and independent states." Within a month, the Continental Congress finally made its decision. It approved one of the world's most important political documents—the Declaration of Independence.

CANADA

Lake
Superior

Lake
Huron

L. Ontario

Lake Erie

(part of
Massachusetts)

N.H.

New
York

Mass.

Boston

Conn.

New York

Rhode
Island

Pennsylvania

Philadelphia

New Jersey

Maryland

Delaware

Virginia

Atlantic
Ocean

North
Carolina

South
Carolina

Georgia

Charleston

	British colonies
✹	Battles of Lexington and Concord

0	100	200 miles
0	100	200 kilometers

Map of the British colonies

DEEP ROOTS OF THE STRUGGLE

Before 1763, most colonists were proud to call themselves British. The settlers who had crossed the Atlantic Ocean had brought their political and social traditions with them. They believed the British government, or **Parliament,** was the best in

American colonists held town meetings in public buildings such as Faneuil Hall in Boston.

the world. They also had developed new freedoms in America.

But things changed after the British won the French and Indian War (1756–1763).

Colonists burned printed matter to protest the Stamp Act.

Although the British had driven the French out of North America, the victory had been expensive. In the future, Parliament said, the American colonies would have to pay more money for the troops that defended them. That money would come from taxes.

The most unpopular new tax law was the Stamp Act, passed in 1765. Every piece of printed material sold in America, including books, news-papers, wills, and playing cards, would be taxed. The Americans quickly protested the Stamp Act.

Few people enjoy paying taxes. But the Americans thought they had a good reason to complain. In Britain, people voted for their representatives in Parliament. These representatives defended the interests of the people who elected them. The Americans had no elected representatives in Parliament, however. The British government was passing tax laws on Americans who had no say in the matter.

Parliament stopped the tax on paper goods. But its leaders refused to give up the right to collect other taxes. It continued to pass new taxes and other laws that limited American freedoms.

TROUBLES IN BOSTON

The colonists who strongly opposed the taxes were sometimes called **Patriots**. Boston, Massachusetts, was one of the centers of Patriot activity. The Patriot leaders there included Samuel Adams and his cousin, John Adams.

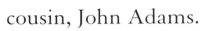

Samuel Adams

John Adams

At times, the protests became violent so the British government put troops in Boston to keep order. Seeing these soldiers, called **redcoats**, only made people even angrier.

12

The Boston Massacre

Patriots disguised as Indians throw tea into Boston Harbor.

In 1770, a local mob clashed with some soldiers. The redcoats fired their guns and killed five people. This event became known as the Boston Massacre.

Bad feelings between the Bostonians and the British grew worse. In 1773, the Patriots decided to protest against the tax on tea. They raided three ships carrying tea in Boston Harbor. The angry

Patriots threw thousands of pounds of the tea into the water. The Boston Tea Party was the first real act of rebellion.

The British Parliament responded with tougher laws. Britain ordered all the colonies to allow British troops to live in houses, inns, and

Colonists were forced to allow British soldiers to live in their homes.

Delegates of the First Continental Congress discuss the issues.

other buildings. More colonists now thought Parliament and King George had gone too far. In September 1774, representatives from the colonies met in Philadelphia at the First Continental Congress to talk about these problems.

16

THE FIRST CONTINENTAL CONGRESS

Some delegates at the Congress did not want to break off their ties with Britain. George Galloway of Pennsylvania wrote a resolution saying that the Americans were "faithful subjects" of King George.

In 1775, Paul Revere rode through the night to warn colonists that British troops were coming.

The resolution failed to pass, but still only a few delegates supported American independence.

The First Continental Congress finally decided that the colonies would cut off all trade with Great Britain unless it ended the tax laws. The representatives also agreed to meet again if another crisis arose. That time came just a few months later—in the spring of 1775.

17

BATTLES AT LEXINGTON AND CONCORD

For the British, Massachusetts was the chief trouble spot. In April 1775, British soldiers were sent to destroy supplies and weapons the colonists had stored for their defense. The soldiers marched from Boston into the countryside. Along the way, they ran into armed colonists. These Massachusetts

A minuteman prepares for battle.

18

In 1775, war broke out between the colonists and the British.

soldiers were called **minutemen**. They got their name because they were supposed to be ready to grab their guns and fight at a moment's notice.

Captain John Parker led a group of minutemen in the town of Lexington. As the redcoats approached, he told his troops "Don't fire unless fired upon, but if they mean to have a war, let it begin here." And so it did.

No one knows who fired the first shot. The minutemen and redcoats exchanged fire in Lexington, and then in the nearby town of Concord. By the end of the day, seventy-three British soldiers and forty-nine colonists were dead.

Massachusetts was in rebellion and the other colonies soon joined it. Another Continental Congress was called to meet in Philadelphia.

20

THE SECOND CONTINENTAL CONGRESS

Thomas Paine

After the battles at Lexington and Concord, the fighting increased. King George stood firm against the colonies. He refused to give in to their demands. As the Second Continental Congress debated what to do, the colonists began to turn against Great Britain.

In January 1776, a small book called *Common Sense* went on sale in Philadelphia. Its author was Thomas Paine. After arriving from England in 1774, he supported the cause of independence.

In *Common Sense*, he spelled out why all Americans should break away from Great Britain.

Paine wrote that King George was a "royal brute [or beast]." He also said that America would achieve greatness only as an independent nation. Paine wrote in a simple style that any reader could understand. *Common Sense* quickly sold more than 100,000 copies. It helped boost the call for independence.

By June 1776, the Second Continental Congress was almost ready to take action. Richard Henry Lee offered his resolution in favor of independence. But some representatives were not ready to vote on it. Some delegates still needed instructions from the leaders of their colonies.

To give members more time, the Congress decided to put off the vote on independence for

COMMON SENSE;

ADDRESSED TO THE

INHABITANTS

OF

AMERICA,

On the following interesting

SUBJECTS.

I. Of the Origin and Design of Government in general, with concise Remarks on the English Constitution.

II. Of Monarchy and Hereditary Succession.

III. Thoughts on the present State of American Affairs.

IV. Of the present Ability of America, with some miscellaneous Reflections.

Man knows no Master save creating HEAVEN,
Or those whom choice and common good ordain.
THOMSON.

PHILADELPHIA;

Printed, and Sold, by R. BELL, in Third-Street,

MDCCLXXVI.

Thomas Paine argued for independence in his book Common Sense.

The Committee of Five

three weeks. During that time, they would choose a committee to write a document. If the Congress voted for Lee's resolution, this document would explain to the world why America was declaring its independence.

24

The committee had five members: Roger Sherman of Connecticut, John Adams of Massachusetts, Robert Livingston of New York, Pennsylvania's Benjamin Franklin, and a tall Virginian named Thomas Jefferson. They were called the Committee of Five.

When they met, they asked Jefferson to be the main author of the **declaration**. "Mr. Jefferson," said John Adams, "had the reputation of a masterly pen."

In addition to his writing skills, Jefferson was a strong believer in independence. Adams also thought it was helpful that Jefferson was from the South. The British would see that all Americans, not only the rebels of Massachusetts, supported independence.

25

WRITING THE DECLARATION

At thirty-three, Thomas Jefferson was one of the youngest delegates at the Second Continental Congress. He was a **scholar** with an interest in arts and sciences as well as politics.

Jefferson wrote his declaration in a rented room. He usually worked standing up and sometimes he worked late into the night. Jefferson also showed his writings to Adams and Franklin. They scribbled notes on the pages and Jefferson added their comments.

Jefferson once said that no one book influenced what he wrote in the declaration. But historians have noted connections between specific writings and Jefferson's work.

Thomas Jefferson writing the Declaration of Independence

A draft of the declaration in Thomas Jefferson's handwriting

A Declaration by the Representatives of the UNITED STATES OF AMERICA, in General Congress assembled.

When in the course of human events it becomes necessary for one people to dissolve the political bands which have connected them with another, and to assume among the powers of the earth the separate and equal station to which the laws of nature & of nature's god entitle them, a decent respect to the opinions of mankind requires that they should declare the causes which impel them to the separation.

We hold these truths to be self-evident; that all men are created equal, that they are endowed by their creator with inherent & inalienable rights; that among these are life, & liberty, & the pursuit of happiness; that to secure these rights, go-vernments are instituted among men, deriving their just powers from the consent of the governed: that whenever any form of government becomes destructive of these ends, it is the right of the people to alter or to abolish it, & to institute new government, laying it's foundation on such principles, & organising it's powers in such form, as to them shall seem most likely to effect their safety & happiness. prudence indeed will dictate that governments long established should not be changed for light & transient causes: and accordingly all experience hath shewn that mankind are more disposed to suffer while evils are sufferable, than to right themselves by abolishing the forms to which they are accustomed. but when a long train of abuses & usurpations [begun at a distinguished period, &] pursuing invariably the same object, evinces a design to reduce them under absolute Despotism, it is their right, it is their duty, to throw off such government & to provide new guards for their future security. such has been the patient sufferance of these colonies; & such is now the necessity which constrains them to alter their former systems of government. the history of the present king of Great Britain is a history of unremitting injuries and usurpations, [among which appears no solitary fact to contra-dict the uniform tenor of the rest [but all have] in direct object the establishment of an absolute tyranny over these states. to prove this, let facts be submitted to a candid world, [for the truth of which we pledge a faith yet unsullied by falsehood]

Dr. Franklin's handwriting

* mr. Adams's handwriting

Another Virginia politician, George Mason, had just written the Virginia Declaration of Rights. Mason said "that all men are by nature free and independent and have certain . . . rights." An earlier British scholar named John Locke

George Mason

influenced both Mason and Jefferson.

In his writings, Locke had discussed the idea of natural laws. According to Locke, these laws, created by God, affect every human being, and every human knows they are true. No one, not even kings, can break these natural laws. Jefferson wrote about natural laws as he drew up the declaration.

On June 28, 1776, the Committee of Five gave Jefferson's work to the Second Continental Congress. The Congress, however, was still not ready to vote. Delegates from Maryland and New York were still waiting to hear from their leaders whether they could vote for independence. The first debate on Jefferson's declaration was put off until July 1.

THE VOTE FOR INDEPENDENCE

When the Continental Congress met again, it got some bad news. Dozens of British ships were now near the coast of New York City. In Charleston, South Carolina, fifty-three British ships patrolled the waters. The delegates faced the threat of an even deadlier war. At the same time, they met to consider Jefferson's declaration and the vote for independence.

The debate that day bored John Adams. What was said "had been repeated . . . in that room before a hundred times, for six months past," he later said. One delegate, however, woke everyone up. John Dickinson of Pennsylvania spoke strongly against independence. "I know the name of liberty is dear

*John Dickinson of Pennsylvania
spoke against independence.*

to each one of us," Dickinson said. "But have we not enjoyed liberty even under the English?"

Adams then stood up to challenge Dickinson. He noted that King George had already said he would not defend the American colonies from outside attack. So Americans were in many ways independent already. Although there is no record of Adams's exact words, Jefferson said that they had "a power that moved us from our seats."

Delegates to the Continental Congress met in this room.

After Adams sat down, the delegates took
a first vote for independence. Nine colonies voted
for it. South Carolina and Pennsylvania voted
against it. Delaware had two delegates—one
voted for and one voted against. The New York
delegates were still waiting for instruction. So the

Congress delayed a final vote for one more day.

This time, on July 2, 1776, the vote for independence was clear. South Carolina and Pennsylvania switched their votes. Though he was dying from cancer, Caesar Rodney, Delaware's third delegate, rode his horse nonstop through the night to break the tie in favor of independence. The New York delegates, who still had not heard from their leaders, did not vote. With the issue of independence finally settled, the Congress turned to Jefferson's declaration.

FINISHING JEFFERSON'S WORK

Jefferson had divided his document into three sections. The first section was a preamble, or introduction. The second included a list of America's complaints against King George. The last part was the Declaration of American Independence. For the first time, the name *United States of America* appeared in a government document.

This famous painting by John Trumbull shows the signers of the Declaration of Independence.

Today, most Americans know the preamble. Jefferson's most famous lines come in the second paragraph: "We hold these truths to be **self-evident**, that all men are created equal, that they are **endowed** by their Creator with certain **unalienable** Rights, that among these are Life, Liberty and the pursuit of Happiness."

Not all the words in the final version were exactly what Jefferson wrote. The Committee of Five had made some changes. And the Continental Congress spent a few days making its own changes. Some parts that might have offended British citizens were taken out. So was a mention of slavery. Finally, on July 4, 1776, the Congress approved the Declaration of Independence.

The signatures on the Declaration of the Independence

John Hancock, the president of the Congress, signed the declaration. The rest of the delegates later signed another copy of the document.

CELEBRATING INDEPENDENCE

The original Declaration of Independence went to a printer. Copies were then sent to all thirteen colonies. The declaration was first publicly read on July 8, 1776. In Philadelphia, John Adams said a festive crowd came to hear the news, and "the bells rang all day and almost all night." Across

The Declaration of Independence is read to the crowds.

Tearing down the statue of King George in New York City

America, people cheered whenever the document was read.

In New York City, when a crowd heard the Declaration of Independence, they knocked down a nearby statue of King George. The metal from the statue was later turned into bullets for General Washington's army.

When the celebrations ended, Americans were citizens of a new country—the United States

39

of America. They knew plenty of hard work remained to be done.

The Continental Congress was now the government of a new nation. It had to try to win help from powerful countries, such as France. It also had to make sure Washington had an army strong enough to fight the British. A long war lay ahead.

During the debates on the declaration, John Adams had written a letter to his wife Abigail. His words expressed what many Americans must have felt after hearing the Declaration of Independence. "I am well aware," he wrote, "of the [work], and blood, and treasure, that it will cost us to maintain this declaration, and support and defend these states. Yet, through all the gloom, I can see the rays of ravishing light and glory."

The original Declaration of Independence is on display in Washington, D.C.

GLOSSARY

colonies—the thirteen British territories that became the United States of America

declaration—an announcement

endowed—given

minutemen—colonists who were ready to grab their guns at a moment's notice

Parliament—the British government

Patriots—American colonists who wanted independence from Britain

redcoats—British soldiers, named after the color of their uniforms

resolution—a statement

scholar—an intellectual, a person who loves learning

self-evident—plain, clear

unalienable—not to be taken away

DID YOU KNOW?

- The basement of Independence Hall was once Philadelphia's dog pound.

- Like other documents of the time, the Declaration of Independence was probably rolled up for storage.

- In 1941, after the Japanese attack on Pearl Harbor, Hawaii, the original Declaration of Independence was moved to a vault in Fort Knox.

- At the National Archives Building in Washington, D.C., the Declaration of Independence is kept in an upright glass and plastic case that has been tested with firearms. It is moved to an underground vault at night.

43

IMPORTANT DATES

Timeline

1763 — Britain defeats France in the French and Indian War.

1765 — Parliament passes the Stamp Act, which taxes colonists on all printed items.

1770 — Five colonists are killed in the Boston Massacre on March 5.

1773 — The Boston Tea Party takes place on December 16.

1774 — The First Continental Congress meets in Philadelphia in September.

1775 — Lexington and Concord battles take place between Massachusetts minutemen and British troops in April.

1776 — The Second Continental Congress meets in Philadelphia on June 7; the Congress votes for independence on July 2 and the Congress approves the declaration on July 4; the declaration is first publicly read on July 8.

IMPORTANT PEOPLE

JOHN ADAMS
(1735–1826), *delegate from Massachusetts, second U.S. president (1797–1801)*

SAMUEL ADAMS
(1722–1803), *leader of the Patriots*

BENJAMIN FRANKLIN
(1706–1790), *delegate from Pennsylvania*

JOHN HANCOCK
(1737–1793), *president of the Continental Congress*

THOMAS JEFFERSON
(1743–1826), *delegate from Virginia at the Continental Congress and author of the Declaration of Independence, third U.S. president from (1801–1809)*

THOMAS PAINE
(1737–1809), *author of Common Sense and other political books*

GEORGE WASHINGTON
(1732–1799), *American general, served as first U.S. president from 1789 to 1797*

WANT TO KNOW MORE?

More Books to Read

Brenner, Barbara. *If You Were There in 1776*. New York: Simon & Schuster Books for Young Readers, 1994.

Fisher, Dorothy Canfield. *Our Independence and the Constitution*. New York: Random House, 1987.

Harness, Cheryl. *Young John Quincy*. New York: Bradbury Press, 1994.

Quiri, Patricia Ryon. *The Declaration of Independence*. Danbury, Conn.: Children's Press, 1998.

On the Web

For more information on this topic, use FactHound.

1. Go to *www.facthound.com*

2. Type in this book ID: 0756500427

3. Click on the *Fetch It* button.

FactHound will find the best Web sites for you.

Through the Mail

National Archives and Records Administration

700 Pennsylvania Avenue, N.W.

Washington, DC 20408

To find out more about the original Declaration of Independence

On the Road

Independence National Historical Park

Visitor Center

3rd and Chestnut Streets

Philadelphia, PA 19106

215/597-8974

To visit where the Declaration of Independence was signed

INDEX

About the Author

Michael Burgan is a freelance writer for both children and adults. A history graduate of the University of Connecticut, he has written more than thirty fiction and nonfiction children's books for various publishers. For adult audiences, he has written news articles, essays, and plays. Michael Burgan is a recipient of an Edpress Award and belongs to the Society of Children's Book Writers and Illustrators.